HOW TO WRITE YOUR PERSONAL HISTORY

HOW TO WRITE YOUR PERSONAL HISTORY

J Malan Heslop
Dell Van Orden

BOOKCRAFT, INC.
Salt Lake City, Utah

Copyright © 1976 by
Bookcraft, Inc.

All rights reserved

No part of this book may be reproduced in any manner whatsoever without written permission from the publisher, except in the case of brief quotations embodied in critical articles and reviews.

Library of Congress Catalog Card Number: 76-40767
ISBN 0-88494-309-7

Lithographed in the United States of America
PUBLISHERS PRESS
Salt Lake City, Utah

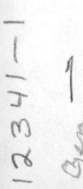

Contents

	Preface	vii
1	Starters, Choose Your Mark	1
2	Freedom in Organizing	7
3	Gathering Remembrances	12
4	Enrich Your Personal History	17
5	It's About You	24
6	When You Start Writing	29
7	Accuracy Is Important	35
8	Day by Day	39
9	Duplicate and Share	43
10	Book of Remembrance	46
	Appendix: Personal History Checklist	49
	Index	55

Preface

The world is full of "would do-ers" — people who would do something if all the conditions were right. "If I had more time," "If I had a place to work," "If I could just write," are some of the excuses.

"Would do-ers" just never seem to get around to writing their personal histories. The difference between somebody who says "I could have" and the person who says "I did" is largely attitude, effort, and the know-how to get the job done.

This book is not only designed to motivate you to start your history but is also a "how-to" book — a book to help you write your personal history.

It's loaded with techniques and procedures on how to organize your material, how to write imaginatively, how to enrich your history, and how to start writing. It's a book filled with examples to help you understand some of the fundamentals which, when applied, will make your personal history readable and valuable.

We stress, however, that there is no special way to write your history. The ideas in this book are merely suggestions, not hard and fast rules. The writing of a history is essentially a personal matter. We don't say, "You must do it this way or that way," or "Your history is incomplete without this or that." A person's creativity and enthusiasm can be killed by locking him into an arbitrary format.

A personal history should be kept simple. It shouldn't become an enslaving monster. It needn't be professionally written, or so highly organized that the effort dies of its own complexity. But within some chosen format everyone should find regular time to digest and then write down what has happened in his life. This will be an enriching experience.

The Prophet Joseph Smith, when the Church was first organized, counseled the members to keep records of the experiences they had, the decisions they made, and the things they learned. The process of keeping records and the use made of them builds people and helps them to grow.

"Who? Me?" is a frequent comment. "I can't write a history about myself." Of course you can. If you can write a letter, you can write your own history. You're the best-known authority on yourself.

Even if you write only a hundred words a day, which is only twelve or thirteen typewritten lines, you will have a volume of about 150 pages, or an average-sized book, within a few months.

We guarantee you a happy experience, and you will be surprised how fascinating your personal history can be.

"How to do it?" That's what this book is all about.

Chapter 1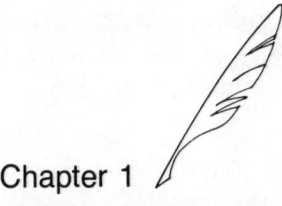

Starters, Choose Your Mark

"A personal history!" you say. "Where do I start?"

There is a choice, depending upon your preference.

You can start at the beginning of your life; that is, you can recall your earliest experiences and begin writing your history from that point.

Alternatively, you can start right now. Write your personal history for today, then continue forward, allowing yourself time to catch up on recording the earlier periods of your life as you go along.

A third method is to organize and write your history according to important events of your life. Using this form, you would write about your athletic experiences, your school years, some phase of your married life, and so on. Each topic would comprise an important chapter of your history.

Remember that your personal history can be written in any order you like — there is no right way or wrong way. Write it in the order that seems best for you at this point. Later you can arrange your material in the desired sequence.

There are many variations of the three general

plans suggested above. The more important thing is *when* you write rather than *how* you write. The time to write is now. Set aside specific periods of time for writing.

If you choose to start by writing the history for the beginning of your life, follow this simple exercise: Think back to the first thing you can remember, your first recollection about your life.

"Well, the first thing I remember," an eighty-three-year-old man said as he started his personal history, "was riding down Ogden Canyon in a wagon with my parents. I was sitting between them on the spring seat. I looked at the cliffs, the high mountains and the big boulders.

" 'Where did they get all the rocks to build this?' I asked. I don't remember the answer, but the question has stuck with me all my life."

Something like that is not a bad start. It opens the memory, and from then on one thought leads to another. It is then easy to go on and recall other early childhood memories. Mental pictures that have long been filed back in the mind now come forward.

"My father was a horse breeder," the man went on, freely recalling early experiences which would become an important part of the chapter on his first years.

Other chapters will readily follow the first as events are recalled. Life is filled with beginnings which impress themselves firmly on the mind. It is simply a matter of recalling and recording. Whether you begin by writing about the first part of your life, a later period, or now, beginnings will stimulate your mind and make the thoughts and the words flow.

The new job you may have started last week is a beginning, an important new chapter in your life. Write about this event while it is fresh in your mind. Such a chapter might even be placed at the start of your personal history, depending upon the influence which that particular beginning has had upon your life.

First-time events are easy to remember, and upon that kind of framework other related events can be built to portray the vivid, often nostalgic, mental pictures you have of those experiences.

"I remember the first time I tried to bake bread," could be the beginning of a chapter. "We had a large wooden flour-bin in the pantry. A spot beneath the lift-up lid was well worn as a result of Mother placing her pan there as she dipped up the flour. I placed my bread pan in exactly the same spot. It was a long reach for me to get the flour because the sack was nearly empty.

"Mother helped me with every step. I was proud to have the flour on my hands. I waited patiently for the bread to rise after we put it on the warming oven above our blue enameled and black iron, wood-burning range. It was a thrill to see the checkered cloth that covered the bread raise up and lift the cloth above the three baking tins.

"The bread was delicious, and the whole family ate it for supper that night."

As your mind opens to recall some of the warm and

wonderful experiences of your life, write them down. Make a long list about those "first-time" experiences.

1. "Long trousers seemed strange the first time...."

2. "The first birthday cake I remember...."

3. "Driving our car for the first time, I...."

4. "It was frightening the first day I went to school...."

5. "My first date turned out to be...."

The list goes on. Start your list immediately. Make notes in your pocket datebook or carry a card or even a used envelope. Put a notebook by your telephone, your favorite easy chair, or a work area. Another good idea is to put a pad of paper and a pencil by your bed. Thoughts may come to you just before you fall asleep or when you awaken. If not recorded, these thoughts can be lost.

The list of beginnings in your life will grow and become an important aid in writing your personal history, however. Do not confine your idea list to beginnings or important events, however. Record what has meaning for you. For example:

1. "I was the only person in our whole town to attend the Chicago World's Fair."

2. "Mother was proud that I was valedictorian of the eighth grade, but I was embarrassed."

3. "Conference at the Mormon Tabernacle was moving."

4. "The price we paid for our 1926 Dodge sedan

cost us the profit from the entire potato crop that year, but it was a beautiful car."

Every person has had many unique experiences. Some are especially memorable. "The way she smiled at me," is one example; or, "When he took my hand...." These moments are significant to you. Others may not have noticed, but you did.

Listing unusual experiences is a way to begin.

1. Humorous events:

"Once I got cotton sandwiches in my lunch. It was April Fool's Day."

2. Sad or tragic events:

"My dog, Lucky, licked my face as I sat on the curb, crying. Our little frame house was burning."

3. Traditional family stories:

"Mother told me that the year I was born...."

4. Important places:

"The big, flat rock near our house was my favorite place to think."

5. Interesting people:

"Gov. William T. Martin invited me into his office the year I won the junior high speech contest.

6. Narrow escapes:

"As the raft drifted toward the flooding river, I knew it would be too late to get off, so I grabbed a limb...."

7. Things I wish had never happened:

"There was no way to replace the lamp I had broken. I apologized again and again, but...."

You may think of other headings for lists that will help as you begin to write your history. Whether it is a story about the first dollar you ever earned or an account of how you got an inside bathroom, put it on your list.

The lists will not only help you to remember but will also help you to organize your personal history.

When lists are used, dates can be more easily attached to events. Calculating dates may require some research, but placing events in the correct time period is worth the effort.

Use the lists as an index and as a record of your writing. Check them off when the chapter is complete.

As this chapter suggests, there are many logical places to start. But there is only one proper time. That time is now.

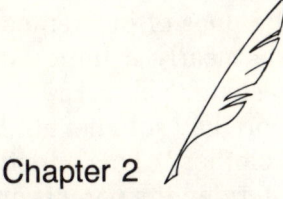

Chapter 2
Freedom in Organizing

Several approaches on how to write a personal history are possible. This allows you freedom in organizing the story. The memory lists that you have prepared will help with the organization of your material.

The most popular way to organize personal histories is the chronological order; you start at the beginning and proceed year by year through your life. The organization is easy and natural.

You will not be able to remember your birth or the very early years, but the information is available through personal interviews and family records. If your mother wrote her personal history, you were probably the subject of an important chapter.

Make your history interesting. Avoid such beginnings as:

"I was born June 18, 1906, the son of Martin and Dorothy Smith Bridgeport, at Westend, Nebraska."

The above information is important, but you can present it in a more interesting way. One possibility is:

"Sand was blowing under the door of our rented home, and the temperature was nearly a hundred degrees on June 18, 1906, at Westend, Nebraska. My mother, Dorothy Smith Bridgeport, had sold her gold ring to buy baby blankets and clothes." This added information could come from interviewing parents or older brothers and sisters.

Here is another way to describe a birth: "There was a celebration at our house the day I was born. I was the first boy in our family. I followed five girls. Father put up a sign, 'It's a BOY' in the front yard and served cookies and punch to all the neighbors. Father was so pleased that he wanted to name me Leonard Wrigley Jones. That was his name. Mother wanted her family represented. Her maiden name was Lorraine Carlson. They named me Carl Leonard Jones. Father had a second celebration at income tax time because I was born December 30, 1947. I provided him with a full deduction for the year."

Following your birth, other experiences can be told in sequence. Tell about your home, play habits, birthdays, and other childhood experiences.

School days open a new era of your life that span several years and bring you to adulthood. During this school period, write about dating, summer fun, employment, travel, church, Scouting, friends, skills, and athletics.

The following is an example: "My senior year in high school was very lonely until I met Lucy Gray, a pretty clarinet player in the school band. I got courage enough to speak to her during the Thanksgiving football game, November 22, 1948. I thought then that I would like to marry her, and I did. But it was five years later."

The chronological order of organization is natural, but variations enliven the narrative. For example, a person could write in one chapter about the six years he spent in the 4-H club. It would not be well to write about the subject six times in a strict chronological pattern.

A combination of chronology and important "life periods" will help your story flow and simplify a complicated subject. We call this grouping. For example, during the childhood period, you could group and write about several incidents pertaining to the apple tree in the back yard:

"It is a wonder I am alive after all the times I fell from that big apple tree in our backyard. I first fell from a box when I was four years old. I was trying to reach a limb. That reach cost me a broken arm. I got a lot of cuts, bruises and scratches from that tree, but the worst fall happened when I was eleven years old and tried to build a tree house. The floor of the house gave way and...."

Other subject groupings follow.

1. Birthdays:

"Mother had a wonderful imagination when it came to birthdays. The year I turned eight, she made a cake eight layers high, but the next year...."

2. Childhood diseases:

"I caught most childhood diseases. When I was three I had the measles; the next year it was chicken pox; and when I was six I had mumps on Christmas Day."

3. Hobbies:

"By the time I was twelve, I had twenty-one dolls of...."

4. Family moves:

"We moved five times by the time I was in the sixth grade, and I can remember every house, every school, and every fight I had."

5. Pets:

"We always had a dog, but...."

6. Vacations:

"Our whole family would pack the station wagon and head for...."

Athletics, dating, cars, trips, and friends are some subjects that can be treated as groupings during your youthful years. Employment, marriage and family, military service, awards, community and Church service, travel, and accomplishment fit well in the adult grouping.

Information may be organized into chronological order within a grouping. Examples are: "The first time I won a tennis match...," or "The hardest job I ever had was my first job. I worked on the...."

Important events are also a basis for organizing your personal history. Groupings in this pattern would include births of children, building houses, appointments to public office, and calls to Church positions.

Choose the way, or combination of ways, that best fits your needs and most applies to you. Then make an outline on paper. As you begin to write, you will have an organizational plan well in mind, and that is always half the battle.

Chapter 3

Gathering Remembrances

One of the best memory-joggers is a box of old photographs or a well-kept scrapbook. Most families have photographs tucked away and unearthing them brings out a flood of memories.

The ideal time to get the most from the photograph box is at a small family gathering. Here a few people can look at the photographs, recall the events, and repeat the stories.

Much history will come from this looking and talking. A notebook or tape recorder is necessary to record the facts, figures, and dates. At the same time, it is a good idea to write the names of persons, dates, and other information on the back of the photograph. A soft, felt-tip pen is best for writing on a photograph. This will not damage the print.

Many new chapters in your personal history will come while you are sorting through the box of photographs.

Be aggressive in suggesting photograph-box gatherings. You may have to ask Aunt Lelila, or some other family member or friend, to bring out her photograph box and share its treasures. Usually, relatives are delighted to comply, and the conversation that follows is a pleasant social activity.

Organized scrapbooks are an even better source of information. Here photographs are often identified by name and date. Photographs and clippings have usually been placed in the scrapbook in some logical order.

Making accurate notes is important. In many cases it is possible to obtain copies of the photographs. Often the negatives, still in the original processing envelope, are in the box, or carefully saved.

It is less expensive to have prints made from the original negative, but if this is not possible photographs can be copied. This, however, takes a photographic skill and close-up equipment, so they should be taken to a professional photographer. A personal family history is enriched by the use of selected photographs.

Interviewing is another valuable technique in gathering information for your personal history. Go to the person who is best informed on the subject. Since parents know most about the circumstances of a birth, conduct an interview with them. An older brother or sister might have valuable information that would enrich your life story. Obviously, when a person cannot remember an event, he must rely on the memory of others. To be accurate, more than one such source of information is necessary. Additionally a check against official records or contemporary journals is desirable.

With a photograph box, information is obtained in a disorganized way, but, with the interview, a high degree of organization becomes possible. First, as the interviewer, you should be prepared with a question outline. It is good to follow the style of a newspaper reporter. Find out *who, what, where, when, why* and *how*. Avoid the cross-examination attitude during an interview. Information flows best when the person being interviewed is relaxed and is in a mood for conversation.

The mood is set by a warm, friendly approach. Most people like to talk in a climate free from pressure. "I suppose you know as much as anybody about . . ." is a good way to start an interview conversation.

Tell the person being interviewed that notes are being taken, and then take notes openly. "I want to remember this just as you say it, so I'm going to take notes. Do you mind?" This will clear the way in just a few words.

Tape recorders are helpful. "Do you mind if I turn my tape recorder on as we talk?" is another way to ensure accurate notes and have the bonus of preserving the story in the person's voice.

While the person being interviewed at first may have some reluctance, knowing that the conversation is being recorded, this attitude usually disappears during a few minutes of warm conversation.

An important rule in interviewing is to let the person being interviewed do most of the talking. Well-prepared, simple questions and a little guidance are all that are necessary in most cases. "What can you remember about Father's old farm up on the Bear River?" may start a conversation that will provide much information. "How did they survive the big

Gathering Remembrances

flood in 1921?" is the type of question which directs the conversation.

Avoid questions that can be answered yes or no. Instead prepare the questions so that an explanation is necessary. If you do receive yes and no answers, follow them up with "why?" or "how's that?" questions.

Where conversation is limited or the ability to answer impaired by a physical disability, you can make statements, giving the person an opportunity to verify the facts with a yes or no, or even a nod of the head. Use caution in not putting words into people's mouths, but let them tell it as it is.

Pictures, scrapbooks or diaries are useful resources when used to guide conversation in an interview. Family records, individual journals, or diaries are excellent sources of information. Many of these are shared, either by the individual, by the family, or by libraries where permission and relationship are provided.

Church or personal records can provide dates and other information. Do not overlook the family Bible, which through the years has been a favorite place to record vital information.

Enrichment for a personal history will come from many persons and places. Be on the alert and be a detective as you discover new information.

This checklist may help in the search for information:

1. Immediate family
2. Close friends

3. Old-timers from the hometown

4. Photograph boxes, scrapbooks and albums

5. Diaries and journals

6. School yearbooks and report cards

7. Scouting and 4-H Club records

8. Church records

9. Deeds and real estate transactions

10. Genealogical and public libraries

11. Newspaper files and back issues

12. Cemeteries

13. Public records

14. Letters, Christmas cards and other greetings

15. The family Bible

Once discovered, information is valuable. Carefully record the date, place, source, and other data, along with the information. This will add validity and make it convenient to return to the source, if necessary. Index the information according to subject and file it for convenience in compiling a personal history.

Gathering, collecting and sorting are an interesting and enjoyable part of writing a personal history. In this way valuable information can be shared with family members and others who are also writing their histories.

Chapter 4
Enrich Your Personal History

Perhaps the greatest enrichment of your personal history comes from those spiritual experiences which strengthen faith and build testimonies. In your recollections of your life there probably are many such experiences.

Significant events, such as when you were baptized, ordained to the priesthood, or received a mission call, should be included in your personal history. Not only should such events be recorded, but you should also verbalize your personal feelings about them. If they occurred some time ago this may take a little memory jogging, but the events and your responses to them are important and should be recorded.

One father who had just ordained his son a deacon recorded his personal feelings in this way:

"When I laid my hands on my son's head, along with the members of the bishopric, I was emotionally moved. Here was my eldest son, and he was receiving the priesthood. I thrilled to know that he was worthy to receive the authority to act in the name of our Heavenly Father, and that he was a good boy and would be an example to his brothers and sisters.

"As I started to speak, my eyes filled with tears and it was difficult for me to talk. When I finished with the ordination, my son stood up and shook hands with the bishopric. He then said to me, 'Thanks, Dad.' It was one of the happiest days of my life, and I drew him close and hugged him. Tears were also in his eyes, and I knew he too was touched by it all."

In addition to these significant ordinances, you've probably had many other kinds of spiritual experiences which should be written into your personal history.

Maybe a particular fast and testimony meeting has uplifted you, or perhaps hearing a new convert speak about her experiences as she joined the Church has enriched you spiritually. It might be that a particular lesson you've taught to your class of eleven-year-olds has been a real, spiritual experience. Write such things down. The best time to record these experiences is right after they occur, while your feelings are still strong and your memory fresh.

Not only is recording spiritual experiences a way to get down on paper some of the important events in your life, but to your children, grandchildren, and others who may read your history it also serves as a testimony of your faith and devotion.

There are several other ways to enrich your history. Some of them are:

1. History of your last name:

For example, if your last name is Haight and your mother's maiden name is Washburn, you might write, "I was the fifth child of William Edward Haight and Dorothy Washburn."

Then start a new paragraph and explain what you know about these names. "The Haight name is of German origin. Due to religious persecution, the Haights fled from the Bohemian forest country to Normandy in the thirteenth century. When they migrated to England, the name was changed for a time to Hoit or Hoyt. After coming to America, in most cases it was changed back to Haight. Nineteen different ways of spelling the name are possible. They include: Hoit, Hoite, Hoyt, Hought, Haight, Hight, Hite, Hyatt, Hayts, Haite, Hayt, and Hait.

"Washburn, also spelled Washburne and Washbourne, was derived from 'wash,' a swift current of a stream, and 'bourne' or 'burne,' meaning a brook."

This type of information is readily available but may require some research. Many published histories of families in America, in Great Britain, and in other countries are available.

The Genealogical Library of The Church of Jesus Christ of Latter-day Saints in Salt Lake City, Utah, contains hundreds of such volumes. In many other areas throughout the world there are branch libraries of the Church, containing books on family history. Public libraries and state historical society libraries may also be valuable sources for this type of information.

2. Background history of your hometown:

"I was born in Idaho Falls, Idaho. The city was originally called Eagle Rock and was founded in 1863 at Taylor's Ferry on the Snake River. The town serviced the heavy traffic on the Salt Lake-Montana road and prospered as a division point on the Utah and

Northern Railway in the 1880s. When the railroad shops were removed to Pocatello, Idaho, fifty miles to the south, in 1887, the town dwindled in population. But it was revitalized in 1890, when it became known as Idaho Falls."

If your hometown is big enough, this type of information can be obtained from an encyclopedia. If it's not listed there, your local library is the best source of information. Books have been published about most cities and towns across America, either by individuals or historical groups. Your public library probably has a copy about your hometown. Your local newspaper is also a good reference source on the history of your town, as their files are usually complete on communities within the area they serve. Many newspapers permit the public to use their files for reference work.

3. Concurrent events in history:

This is where your own personal history can include significant national, international, or community happenings that occurred on the same days or within the period of time you are writing about.

"The Davenport, Iowa Ward was reorganized on Sunday, July 20, 1969, and I was sustained as first counselor in the bishopric. This was the same day that man first walked on the moon. We arrived home from sacrament meeting just in time to watch it on television. Although the live pictures were blurry, it was a thrill to see Neil A. Armstrong step down the ladder from the spacecraft and become the first man on the moon.

"After the telecast, I walked outside and looked at the moon. It was a full moon and shone brightly. I remember saying to myself, 'There's actually a man from earth walking around on the moon right now.' Then I thought, 'All that I can see in the heavens are God's creations,' and it made me realize more fully how insignificant man really is when compared to God."

Again your local newspaper is the best source of concurrent events. Most daily newspapers have past editions of their newspapers on microfilm, which they usually permit the public to use. Weekly newspapers are not usually a source of reference for events of national and international significance happening concurrently, but are invaluable when it comes to community and small-town news. These events can also be tied in with your personal history.

In writing about concurrent events of your life, don't overlook the advertisements in the newspapers. It is interesting to record details about popular merchandise, including price, since such details will change radically during your life.

"When I was born in 1928, bacon was selling for thirty-two cents a pound in Salt Lake City, fresh salmon for twenty-five cents a pound, cinnamon rolls, made with milk and eggs, were twenty cents a dozen, and ice cream sodas, all flavors, were ten cents.

"A four-door, six-cylinder Dodge sedan was $895; a baby grand piano, with a bench to match, was $399; and a three-piece bedroom set was $48. A one-month's subscription to the daily newspaper was sixty cents."

4. Background information on the company you work for or have worked for:

"For twenty years, I worked as a machinist for Smedley and Co. Smedley's was the original machine shop in Thompson Falls, Nevada. It was started by two brothers, Earl and Jim Smedley, in 1954. I had gone to school with them, and after we graduated from high school they started the company and asked that I come to work for them. My primary responsibility was to take a blueprint of a machine part and, from that design, cut the part out on a lathe. I made a lot of parts for cars and airplanes. The work was fascinating because I felt that I was creating something with my hands."

There are many other ways to enliven your personal history. For instance, since each chapter should have a heading or title, use variety in these chapter headings. If you have a spiritual chapter, use a spiritual heading. For a light, carefree chapter use a zippy heading. Keep in mind, however, that chapter headings should convey what the chapter is about. Don't get too cute and miss the message of the chapter.

Photographs can also be included in your personal history. If you talk about your first home, include a picture of that home in your history. If you were on the championship football team, you might include a picture of that team. Charts and maps too are good for illustrations.

For completeness, you might try indexing your history. It's not difficult, although it will take some time. Buy a supply of three-by-five-inch index cards or tear

Enrich Your Personal History

sheets of paper into an appropriate size. Use one card or piece of paper for each idea, word, or name you index. Write this entry on the card or paper, followed by the page number in your history on which it is found. For example: "Peters, John L., 10."

There are two basic types of indexes. A simple one just lists words and the page numbers like this:

> Priesthood, 12, 21, 55

The more informative type appears something like this:

> Priesthood, source of strength, 12
>   blessings of, 55
>   ordination to, 21

Which one you choose is an individual matter, but the second clearly is more valuable, particularly since on some basic subjects (as in the above example) you may have several cards on one subject. Don't try to get more than one *page* entry on any one card.

After you have gone through your history, writing the index details on the cards, arrange the cards in alphabetical order. Do whatever editing is necessary.

Now, you're ready to type the index. Just type the information from the cards onto sheets of paper, which are the same size as others in your personal history. Insert these pages at the back of the book.

As you enrich your history you'll find that the people and places come alive, and your history takes on a new dimension. In addition it's fun. Both the doing and the result will be well worth the additional effort.

Chapter 5
It's About You

There are many moments of truth when it comes to writing your personal history. To reflect on your past and to take a close look at your present could be an exercise in mixed emotion.

Certainly, you will want to present your best image, but you should also share with readers a few knocks and a few regrets. The important thing is to make your story real, to present your true self. Talk about your emotions and your struggles. Tell of overcoming weaknesses and frustrations. But also talk about your accomplishments. Brag a bit, if you have something to brag about. The rule is not to overdo any of them.

Your history should be a work of personal literature. It should tell the story of you. Prayerfully and thoughtfully written, it should be a strength to the writer and to the reader. Remember, histories are written for those who follow. Your history will be cherished by your children and grandchildren. If it presents the true you, it will be preserved for generations to come.

Tell your true feelings:

"I fretted a great deal about having a big nose. I

didn't realize that I had a big nose until about the fourth grade, when someone called me 'big nose.' From then on I grew very conscious of my nose. It was really a struggle during the years I was young. I didn't think the boys liked me, and I wasn't the most popular girl in school. I think now that others didn't notice my nose, but I worried. In my adult life I realize that my fears were silly because a wonderful man, handsome — and with a small nose — did fall in love with me."

Examine your present life as a product of your earlier experiences:

"The most rewarding experience in leadership happened to me when I was fifteen years old. I was assigned as a camp counselor, and I stayed in the counselors' cabin with several other boys. The camp director taught us some principles of leadership. I can still remember some of them but, even more important, I felt a satisfaction in being a leader. Now, as chairman of the board of directors of the Cheeney Company, the second largest distributing company in the country, I still look back on those early experiences and the basic leadership principles learned there."

Recognize how events altered the course of your life:

"I always wanted to be a forest ranger, but I ended up being a farmer. We had always lived on a farm, and I enjoyed farming. I was a good farmer, but I started out to be a forest ranger. I had to make a choice of serving a mission or going to forestry school. My parents did not have enough money for both. I chose the mission. I have no regrets, but I still like the smell of pine trees."

Not everything is easy in one's life, and the struggles and discouragements can paint the picture of life as it is.

"I went to church alone for twenty years. Oh, I took the children, but when I say alone, I mean George didn't go. He believed in God, but he wouldn't go to meetings.

"I tried everything I could, but it took our neighbor, Bill Gnadt, to get him to see the light. Now George is a Sunday School teacher in his 'old age.' I am proud of him, but I feel that those twenty years could have been tremendously important in our development."

Some deep regrets may find a place in a personal history. A happy ending helps, but that is not always possible:

"I curse the day I took my first drink. I hadn't meant to, but . . . ," or, "I guess I was extra ambitious because I didn't see the harm in working two jobs to get the things we wanted."

A personal characteristic may reveal you to your readers:

"My quick temper got me in trouble more than once," or, "I just couldn't stand to be outdone, but I learned a good lesson when. . . ."

Someone might write: "I fought every kid in school until I learned there were better ways to make friends. Maybe it was that little kid that knocked my socks off over at Riley School that taught me a lesson."

Mistakes are made in life. Many marriages end in divorce, and this too becomes part of a personal history. "Lois and I tried very hard, but there were some differences that we could not resolve. I think that, if I had spent more time with her and the children, things would have been different."

Another experience might be written in this way. "It took many years to heal the wounds when John left our home. I think we both tried for a successful marriage, but our goals were different. I hope he found the things he wanted."

Other disappointing or even tragic events should be part of a personal history:

"What started out to be a wonderful vacation, ended in tragedy for our family when...."

"We borrowed heavily, thinking that the land deal would go through with Ajax Company. The president of the company disappeared and we lost everything."

"I shall never forget Jenny's sweet spirit. I cried for weeks after she died. I think I still cry inside because it was sad to lose her at such a young age. She was...."

Success belongs in all lives. Everyone achieves something in his own plane of activity. It doesn't hurt to brag a little. But it should be done in good taste, as illustrated in the following examples:

"You can't imagine the satisfaction we had when Ruth was chosen to represent her class at...."

"Roger worked for years before he was able to make the first team. His dedication paid off though, because he was high point man in most of the games. When he graduated...."

"I have kept a scrapbook of all the awards that Bill and Mary received. Music seemed to come naturally to them, and, of course, they had lessons from...."

List accomplishments, explain successes, attribute ability, and recognize the help of others as you write about the positive things of your life.

Your life's history is a prime opportunity to express and teach your philosophy. Much of your life will speak for itself through your record. But you would be lax if you failed to testify of the truths that you know:

"I think work has been the prime factor in my life. My father taught me to work, and I have learned that comparatively few are willing to work extra hard for success."

"Family togetherness has been my pet philosophy. From the time the children were very small, we have...."

"I don't think I could have enjoyed the happiness I have had in my life, if it were not for a strong belief in God, and the privilege of talking to him in prayer. I have a testimony that...."

"I want my children to know the great blessings that their mother gave to them. I lived with her for fifty-two years and...."

"Let me reinforce my belief in...."

Be honest with yourself. Share the difficult with the good. By your example you can build those that follow.

Chapter 6

When You Start Writing

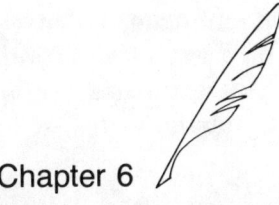

When you start writing your personal history develop your own style of writing. Don't try to be a Hemingway or a Faulkner; just be yourself.

There is no right or wrong way to write your history. As long as your history reflects your personality and your feelings and describes your life experiences, that's what counts. There are, however, some ideas which can improve your writing, make it more interesting and readable.

An easy way to be yourself is to write as you talk. One technique is to ask yourself, "Now, if I were to tell my next-door neighbor about myself, how would I begin?"

You don't beat around the bush when you talk with a friend. You instinctively slice through to the heart of the matter. Good writing is like that too.

It would be a mistake to have your history sound like a college term paper, if you don't talk that way. To make your history "you," it must be written in your words — not somebody else's.

Let your imagination run. This doesn't mean you

need to fabricate something that isn't true. To write imaginatively is to be colorful and descriptive as you put your thoughts on paper. As you write, use words that conjure up sights, sounds, smells, tastes, and sensations.

Don't write, "I was born in a big house." That's too general and not very interesting. Instead, describe the "bigness." "I was born in a two-story house that was the highest house on the whole street. My dad had a sixteen-foot ladder that just barely reached the eaves of the roof...."

This paints a word picture. The reader not only knows how high the house is but can also see, in his mind's eye, a whole row of houses. Your house, with a ladder leaning against it, is jutting above the others.

If you are describing your early home life and the homemade bread your mother used to bake, don't just say: "I remember my mother's home-baked bread. It always smelled so good." Here the word picture is almost nonexistent.

Try writing it like this: "I remember coming home from school on crisp fall days and walking through the back door. The warm smell of freshly baked bread tantalized my cold nose, and I could hardly wait to get my coat off and have a hot, thick slice smothered in butter and honey."

What young person hasn't experienced that feeling? Capture it on paper, and you have the ingredients of a fascinating personal history.

To write descriptively isn't a matter of learning grammar, although there are rules which will make your writing more readable. To write descriptively is to develop the ability to put your feelings on paper. When writing, many people freeze up, and their writing becomes stifled. Their personal histories prove uninteresting.

Practice writing imaginatively. Write down a subject topic from your recollections: "When I was a kid, my favorite ice cream was chocolate raspberry."

Make a list of all the things you remember about chocolate raspberry ice cream and the store where you bought it. The list might go something like this:

1. "On hot, summer days, my sister and I would each have a nickel to spend for ice cream."

2. "On the big board in the ice cream shop, there were so many flavors to choose from. I think there must have been twenty-five or thirty."

3. "I remember choosing chocolate raspberry because it sounded so funny."

4. "What a delightful surprise when I took the first lick. It tasted so good." (Now, carry that another step. Why did it taste so good?) "It was so cool," or maybe, "It reminded me of a raspberry patch in the summer." If you will try, those early memories locked in your mind will come. Put them down on the list.

5. "Mr. Smitz, the owner, said I was the funniest kid around because I always ordered the same flavor."

Write down all the things you can remember, no matter how incidental you think they are. Once you have completed your list, start to compose them into sentences and paragraphs, eliminating the superfluous items. It may take a little practice and perfecting, but you're on your way to writing imaginatively.

One of the keys to descriptive writing is the use of vigorous, vivid verbs. For example, if you work in a factory, don't write it, "The factory operates seven days a week," but rather, "The factory hammers away seven days a week." The "hammers away" conjures up a mental image.

Verbs, which provide direction for sentences, are among the strongest parts of speech, but most people writing their personal histories fall into the habit of using easy verbs. Use the right verb to describe the action; that is, use strong verbs to portray action that is strong, weak verbs for weak action.

Other "rules" to make your history more readable and interesting include:

1. Avoid the overuse of starting off a sentence with "I," or "my." It is easy to begin a sentence with: "My dog was named Spot," "My room was in the attic," "I was the fifth child," "I learned to drive," "I overcame my doubts," etc. (Too frequently beginning a sentence with "I" and "my" will give your writing a feeling of repetition, which creates monotony.)

2. Keep your sentences and paragraphs short. This will brighten your history considerably. Long sentences and paragraphs are too hard to digest. A short, simple, conversational style is better.

3. Avoid so-called "elegant" words when simple ones will do just as well. *Died* is better than *passed away* or *succumbed; fire* is better than *conflagration;*

When You Start Writing

burned to the ground is better than *destroyed by fire*.

4. Explain terms which may be unfamiliar to those who read your history. You may know the meaning of words you use, but will your grandchildren? For example, if you're a railroad worker, you may use the term *gandy dancer* in your history, but most people don't know it is a laborer on a section gang. Explain it.

5. Avoid the frequent use of cliches. There are hundreds of trite phrases that have been used over and over again. How many times have you heard: hangs in the balance, fell like a lead balloon, nipped in the bud, a super-human effort, the old college try, threw in a monkey wrench? If you frequently use these and other cliches in your history, it will make your writing trite and uninteresting. Consider the following sentence, for example: "Running neck and neck with Westlake's best sprinter, I gave it a super-human effort and crossed the finish line just ahead of him."

Why is a close race always "neck and neck"? Why is great effort always "super-human," and why do runners always "cross the finish line"?

Here is a more descriptive way to portray the race.

"Through the sweat running down my face, I could see the tape across the track just ahead. My lungs were burning. I could hardly breathe. My legs ached. I knew Westlake's sprinter was just behind me. I could hear his heavy breathing, drawing closer. I could hear the slap of his feet every time they hit the track — louder and louder. Gasping to breathe, I lunged forward, feeling the tape snap as it creased my chest."

Whether you write your history in longhand or on the typewriter is a personal choice. Typewritten histories are easier to read, but longhand reveals much about the writer and his personality. The use of a cassette tape recorder to record thoughts and feelings is another consideration, but this involves transcribing the material, which is a laborious task.

The important thing is to start to write. We repeat, there is no right way or wrong way. For you, there's only your way. Write whatever comes to your mind. You can go back and rewrite and rework the writing later, but for now capture those feelings, those smells, those sounds, those sights, and those events that you remember.

That's what a personal history is all about.

Chapter 7

Accuracy Is Important

Take the time to be accurate when you're researching and writing your personal history. There is no valid excuse for misinformation and error.

Errors creep in when people hurry unreasonably or when they're inattentive. When you're working on your personal history, do it at a time when your mind is alert. Don't try to sandwich it in after you've worked twelve or fourteen hours and are exhausted.

Avoid distractions. If you're constantly being disturbed by children running in and out of the house or the blaring of the television set or radio, you're taking a chance with the accuracy of your history. Work alone, where you can devote some uninterrupted time to writing.

Remember, the place and time do make a difference when it comes to writing your history. The place should be conducive to quiet reflection. In all probability, you'll have to schedule the time; it won't just happen. As you plan your day's activities, plan for some time to work on your personal history.

Your history is a written record of your life. It's invaluable. An example of the value one family placed on its family history was clearly emphasized during the 1972 flood in Rapid City, South Dakota. Before a devastating flood hit, wiping out a third of the city, families along the river were given some warning that there might be high water if the rains continued to fall in the Black Hills above the city. Families were told they should evacuate to higher ground.

One family living in a luxurious two-story home, furnished with fine furniture worth several thousand dollars, had little trouble in deciding what to take with them. They had been in previous disasters before — an earthquake in California and a tornado in the Midwest. They knew what could be replaced. The family loaded their children into the car and took with them only their personal records — irreplaceable pictures, personal histories, and genealogy records.

The value of a personal history, however, is lessened if it's inaccurate. The spelling of names is important. The rule of thumb is: "Don't assume you know how to spell a name." There are just too many ways to spell names. Is it Lyn, Lynn, or Lynne? Is it Smith, Smithe, Smyth, or Smythe? They could all be pronounced the same.

Telephone books and city directories are valuable sources for proper spellings of names. Back issues of newspapers can also be helpful if you know the date or period of time when the name appeared, though name spellings will often be less reliable in a newspaper than in a more permanent publication.

Dates are also important, but they cause many er-

Accuracy Is Important

rors in personal histories. A simple thing like hitting the wrong key on the typewriter can cause an error without your even knowing about it. Be sure to read your material after you've typed it. If you are using dates and ages together, check them against each other. If you say, "On my fortieth birthday on April 22, 1976," check to see that you have April 22, 1936, as your birthdate. Check and double check. You could catch some easily made mistakes, such as the common one of recording a child as born when his mother is only seven years old or so.

Don't assume you know how to spell every word you'll have to use. If you have any doubts, refer to the dictionary. A dictionary should be a standard reference tool when you write. Remember that what you write is a positive or negative reflection of you. Names of places can be checked in an atlas or gazetteer, or on a map. Once again, don't assume.

As you interview people for your personal history, you may receive two different sets of "facts." If so, you need to verify which (if either) is right. A woman who was the youngest of several children started to write her history after she was fifty years old. Her parents were both dead, so she interviewed two of her older sisters for facts about her early childhood. But they gave conflicting information about her birth and young years. If such a thing happens to you, conduct additional interviews with other people as necessary to get the right story.

As you interview, always ask the person where he or she received the information. Avoid hearsay. If the information has been handed down from generation to generation, state that in your history.

One example might be: "According to our family tradition, my great-great-grandfather, Abel Knight, spent many hours listening to the Prophet Joseph Smith expound on the scriptures while at the temple site in Nauvoo, Illinois. My father said that, as a young boy, his father would sit by the old coal stove at night, after the chores were done, and tell of the experiences of his grandfather in Nauvoo."

This type of information is interesting, but you may not be able to verify it. By writing it in this way, however, you attribute it to family sources and state that it is information passed down from other generations.

After you have finished your history, have someone outside of your family read it over. Oftentimes a writer or his family is too close to his work to spot the errors. Having someone else read it is a good way to assure accuracy.

Chapter 8
Day by Day

History is known by many only when it is recorded. Important events can happen, but, unless they are preserved and shared, they will not be a part of written history. Events that seem routine today may be important at some time in the future. Your personal history is a record of day-by-day happenings. In keeping a personal journal, you are recording that history.

The best and most accurate record is one that is written every day. It is surprising how facts can become scrambled only a few days later. It is difficult to remember the sequence of events even for a week. A familiar thought process of someone trying to remember back even one week might go like this. "Let's see, did the letter come last Wednesday or was it Thursday? Maybe it was even Tuesday."

Admittedly there may be periods in your life when no significant events happen, but even the absence of activity may be worth noting.

A goal of writing a few lines every day is realistic. Writing only when important things happen will lead to neglect. The very process of deciding what is important is eliminated when a record is made every day.

A personal journal must become a habit. Choose a special time, probably at the close of each day, and write a few lines as needed.

Consider these additional guidelines:

1. *Don't be repetitious.* You would not write, "I went to work" each day. You could write: "I started a new job today at the post office. I will be in the package department at first. Most of the day was spent in training."

As significant changes are made in your employment or in other routine activities, make a note of the changes. "I was transferred to the letter department. . . ." Record the interesting, significant, or unusual events of each day in your daily journal. "I was ill and did not go to work . . . ," or "A new foreman was hired today."

2. *Write in a concise way.* Avoid trite statements and excessive words. You should not write, "Dear Diary, today I take my pen in hand and write of the beauties of spring." Instead you could write, "The cherry tree today is loaded with blossoms."

3. *Be sure of proper identification.* Use a person's full name the first time he is mentioned in connection with an event in your life. You can then use his first or last name in following references. "George W. Harper, personnel manager at Swift Airline Company, is my partner for the golf match. George won the public parks meet last year."

The same is true of addresses and other information. Don't write, "We stopped at Columbus today to see Thelma on the way to the reunion." This is incomplete. It should be recorded, "On the way to the Bitton reunion in Smithfield, Idaho, we stopped at Columbus, Montana, today to see our friend, Thelma Pace, who was my roommate in college." These identifying facts may be well known to you at the time you write them, but if you try to remember them years later they may be uncertain.

4. *Use direct quotes when appropriate.* While important events are happening, take notes so that you will have the exact words. If you rely on memory, the words will slip away and be lost.

Many people use tape recorders to record exact words when awards are being made. Direct quotes during such moments will make your day-by-day journal interesting and more valuable. "The mayor handed the award to our son, Jeff, and said, 'This is a sparkling young man. I do not recall anyone who worked so well with such a happy spirit.' "

5. *Record your personal impressions and feelings as they happen.* Write while your feelings are fresh. "It seemed wrong to me that . . . ," or "I was moved to tears by the devotion of the people. . . ."

6. *In your daily journal, include the important happenings in local and world events.* It will add to your personal history to write, "I ran out of gas today, but the U.S. astronauts had more success. They landed on the moon for the first time."

7. *Expect that someone else may read your daily journal.* If you have some very personal and intimate things to record, you may choose to have a separate journal for them. Letters written each day, while

you're on a trip or in the military service, should be saved as part of a journal.

Keeping a daily journal requires dedication. It is a worthy project that should be entered into early, seriously, and with lifetime commitment.

Though in reality the journal is itself a personal history, from time to time you may want to condense its contents and compile a separate smaller history. This procedure would make your daily journal more or less the source material for a personal history beyond the point at which you compiled a history of the past and commenced a daily journal.

A daily journal, faithfully kept, will prove valuable in many ways and interesting to you and others. It will help to secure your place in history.

Chapter 9

Duplicate and Share

When you've completed your history to the current period of your life, what are you going to do with it? The best idea is to share it.

Give a copy of your personal history to members of your family. This necessitates some type of duplication. The choices range from making office machine copies to having the manuscript professionally printed and bound in book form.

For most people, the professionally printed and bound route is ruled out by the high cost. Inflation has hit the printing industry like every other business. Costs of paper alone are extremely high. Additional expenses involved are typesetting, picture processing, and printing and binding the book.

If cost is not a determining factor for you, though, you may want to travel first-class and produce a professional-looking book. In that case, be sure to get bids from two or three printing firms. Tell them what you want, including how many books you want printed, and they will give you a price. Knowing the total cost and the number of books to be printed, you can easily figure the cost per book — which on small jobs, like printing personal histories, will be high.

A more practical method of duplication, and one which more easily fits the average budget, is quick printing at a commercial firm. Such firms do quality work, giving you an excellent reproduction of your material as submitted at a cost considerably less than that of a regular print job. By checking under the heading "Printers" in the yellow pages you should be able to come up with the names of several quick-printing firms, depending upon the size of your city. Usually quick printers duplicate by offset, a quality type of printing.

The difference between a commercial printing company and a quick-print operation is basically that a quick-print firm takes your material as is and duplicates it without changes. In the quick-print business, the material you submit must be "camera ready." No additional type will be set, no pictures will be processed. The finished copy will look exactly the same, including smudges and errors, as the original. This is why accuracy is so important. Once the sheet is duplicated, it becomes the finished product.

When you begin to type your manuscript, make sure you have a new ribbon in your typewriter. A new ribbon makes the characters sharp and clear, eliminating many of the problems of hard-to-read duplicated copies.

Have some fun with your manuscript as you make it camera ready. If you have a flair for art, you might add some illustrations. But be sure to use strong colors for duplication since the process will reproduce only in a single color, which you almost certainly will want to be black (on white paper). A simple black and white illustration reproduces best. Blues and yellows are extremely difficult to pick up by a duplicating process.

You can also add interest by lettering the chapter titles, rather than typing them. By lettering, you can make the words larger, giving more impact to the chapter headings. Letter first in pencil to make sure you get what you want, and then go over it with black ink. Be careful with erasures; they create smudge marks which can be picked up in the duplication process.

An even less expensive method of duplication, but also one of poorer quality, is achieved with office machine copies. Commercial firms duplicate, using office machines, for a few cents a sheet. As with quick-printing, you get exactly what's on the page you're duplicating.

One advantage the quick-print and office machine copying has over a bound book is that you can add to your history. If you put your history in a three-ring binder or a standard genealogy book, it is a simple matter just to add another sheet to update it. No additions can be made to a bound book.

No matter which way you choose — and you should consider the alternatives carefully, weighing need and cost — it's wise to duplicate your history. You have many family members interested in receiving a copy. Share it with them.

Chapter 10

Book of Remembrance

A written personal history is only a part of the book of remembrance, the master volume of your life. A proper book of remembrance not only includes a well-prepared personal history but also involves a much broader scope of material such as family group sheets, pedigree charts, photographs, certificates, maps, letters, and other significant documents.

Just as the writing of a personal history requires time and careful consideration, so a book of remembrance takes a lifetime of collecting, selecting, and preparing. Compiling the book of remembrance is a subject that deserves a much fuller treatment than can be given here, where we consider it only as it applies to a personal history.

There are at least three different ways to include your personal history as part of your book of remembrance: (1) at the beginning or the end of the book; or (2) dispersed throughout the book; or (3) as a separate volume. How it is done is a matter of personal choice.

Frequently the personal story relates directly to the material in the book of remembrance. If this is so in your case, you may want to make your history an integral part of your book of remembrance. For example, if that book includes several pictures of you as a child, you could include the story of your childhood from your personal history opposite or near the photo pages. Alternatively, you could have three or four photographs on the same page and the history written around them. Similarly, if you have pictures of your grandchildren, you may want to include your written history about each child on opposite pages or near the photographs.

How you place your personal history in your book of remembrance also depends on how you have decided to have your history duplicated. Office machines will not make good reproductions of photographs, certificates, or other documents. If you have chosen this duplication process, you may want to have one volume for your history and a separate volume for photographs, certificates, and other documents.

Frequently a book of remembrance may itself become the basis for writing a personal history, since people usually save pictures, clippings, certificates, and awards, and these can serve as memory joggers as a person starts to write his history. In fact, a person with not much more than a box or envelope full of pictures plus a few bits and pieces of information may find that the best way to plan and write his personal history is to use a well-organized book of remembrance as a guide.

It is well to determine which system you prefer before you start on the final draft of your personal history. Page size, format, and style of the history should conform to your book of remembrance if the history is to be included in the same binder.

Your book of remembrance is the documented history of your life. In one form or another it should include a well-written personal history.

Appendix
Personal History Checklist

I. Preparation
    A. Collecting and filing material
        1. diaries and journals
        2. interviews
        3. clippings
        4. photographs
        5. documents
        6. other
    B. Idea lists and background material
        1. childhood
            a. earliest memories
            b. play activities
            c. pets
            d. first experiences
            e. people
        2. youth
            a. new experiences
            b. school
            c. friends
            d. Scouting, 4-H, other activities
            e. hobbies
            f. sports
            g. accidents and close calls
            h. first money earned

                i. trips
        3. adult
            a. pre-marriage
                new responsibilities
                automobiles
                music
                dating
                Church advancements
                school accomplishments
                college
                mission
                hobbies
                employment
                travel
            b. courtship and marriage
                social life
                dating and choosing
                wedding
                honeymoon
                finances
                first home
                children
                challenges
                successes
                frustrations
                special moments
                Church service
                community service
                sports
                people
                spiritual and other special experiences
                sickness and accidents
                gardens and landscape
                art and music

Personal History Checklist

        honors and awards
        current important historical events
        pets
        organizations
        writing, published and unpublished
        genealogy
   c. family
        children: birth, characteristics, growth
        book of remembrance
        special problems
        parents
        grandparents
        family homes
        vacations
        family meetings
        genealogy
        cooperation in family
        responsibilities
        work assignments
        accomplishments and awards
        speeches given
        family policy
        job hunting
        education
        family hobbies and activities
4. important life periods
   a. military service
      branch
      memorable experiences
      war
      rank
   b. Church mission
      area called to
      successes

       people
       growth
       testimony
  c. higher education
     school selected
     subjects studied
     social life
     accomplishments
     sports
     cultural arts
     people
     teachers
     graduation
  d. employment
     searching for work
     skills
     promotions
     accomplishments
     background of company
  e. homes
     location
     style
     cost
     gardens
     neighbors
     community
     shopping
     upkeep
     sale and moving
     furniture
     problems
  f. Church activity
     offices held
     teaching experiences

Personal History Checklist

    new chapel
    welfare projects
    athletics and activities
    responsible positions
    blessings
    ordinations
    spirit of people
    spiritual experiences
   g. political and community activity
    service given
    offices held
    interesting politics
    people
    conventions and elections
 C. Search and research
  1. church records
  2. public records
  3. libraries
  4. newspaper files
  5. personal interviews
  6. others

II. Organization
 A. Determine plan
  1. strict chronology
  2. chronology by subject
  3. important events
  4. combination

III. Writing
 A. Commitment to start
  1. goal is _____
 B. Honest writing
  1. be yourself
  2. write the things you know
  3. identify hopes and dreams

    C. Cover the subject
        1. who
        2. what
        3. where
        4. when
        5. why
        6. how
    D. Assure accuracy
        1. spelling of names and places
        2. dates
        3. spelling
        4. grammar
        5. read through for accuracy
IV. Enrichment
    A. Current history added
    B. Background information
    C. Illustrations
        1. photos
        2. diagrams
        3. maps
V. Duplicate and Print
    A. Copy prepared
        1. attractive
        2. free from error
    B. Number of copies needed
    C. Publication cost available

Index

A

Accomplishments, writing about, 24; listing of, 28
Accuracy, efforts for, 35
Advertisements, 21

B

Beginnings, life filled with, 2; impressed on mind, 2; mind stimulated by, 3; listing of, 4; avoidance of certain, 7
Bible, source of information, 15
Birth, remembering, 7; experiences following, 8; interviewing parents about, 13
Book of Remembrance, compilation of, 46; documented history, 48

C

Charts, use of, 22
Checklist, personal history, 49
Cliches, avoidance of, 33

D

Dates, attached to events, 6; important, 36
Diaries, useful resources, 15
Dictionary, for reference, 37
Distractions, avoidance of, 35
Duplication, of history, 43; types of, 43-45; practical method of, 44

E

Enrichment, for history, 15, 18; greatest, 17
Errors, no excuse for, 35; check for, 38
Events, important, 1; first time, 3; humorous, 5; sad, tragic, 5, 27; basis for organizing, 10, 39; significant, 17; concurrent, 20
Experiences, earliest, 1; making list of, 4; unusual, 5; childhood, 8; spiritual, 17, 18

F

Feelings, true, 24; recording of, 31, 41
Freedom, in organizing, 7

G

Groupings, types of, 9-10
Guidelines, for writing, 40

H

Headings, for chapters, 22
Hearsay, avoidance of, 37
Hobbies, writing about, 16
Hometown, background of, 19

I

Ideas, making list of, 4
Identification, proper, 40
Illustrations, use of, 22, 44
Imagination, use of, 29

Impressions, recording of, 41
Index, using lists as, 6; according to subject, 16; for completeness, 22; types of, 23
Interview, with parents, 13; avoiding cross-examination in, 14
Interviews, personal, 7

J

Journal, for others to read, 41; writing requires dedication, 42
Journals, source of information, 15

L

Library, Genealogical, 19
List, of experiences, 4
Lists, headings for, 6; as index, 6; memory, 7; of things remembered, 31

M

Manuscript, when typing, 44
Maps, use of, 22
Memories, flood of, 12
Mental pictures, in mind, 2; portrayed, 3
Methods, writing, 1

N

Name, last, history of, 18
Names, checking spelling of, 36
Newspapers, reference source, 20; source of concurrent events, 21; advertisements in, 21
Notebook, use of, 4, 12
Notes, recording of, 4; important, 13; taking of openly, 14

O

Order, chronological, most popular, 7; natural, 9
Ordinances, recording of, 18

P

Parents, interviewing of, 8
People, interesting, 5
Pets, writing about, 10
Philosophy, personal, 28
Photographs, tucked away, 12; can be copied, 13; enriching history by, 13, 22; in Book of Remembrance, 47
Places, important, 5

Q

Questions, type of, 15
Quotes, direct, use of, 41

R

Recollections, first, 2
Repetition, avoidance of, 40
Research, a possible requirement, 19

S

Scrapbooks, source of information, 13; useful resource, 15
Sentences, length of, 32
Sequence, desired, 1; experiences told in, 8
Spelling, names, 36
Stories, family, 5
Style, writing, 29
Successes, writing about, 27; explaining of, 28

T

Tape recorder, use of, 12, 34, 41; helpful to use, 14
Terms, explaining of unfamiliar, 33
Testimonies, building of, 17
Thoughts, recording of, 4
Time, to write, 2, 6; best, for recording, 18

V

Vacations, writing about, 10
Variations, to beginning, 1
Verbs, use of vigorous, 32

W

Weaknesses, writing about, 24
Words, use of own, 29
Writing, no right or wrong way, 1, 29, 34; developing style of, 29; colorful, 30; practicing imaginative, 31; quiet place for, 35; guidelines for, 40